RESEARCH

PRESENTS

THE AMAZING TRANSFORMATIONS OF TOM TERRIFIC

By Kevin Scott Collier

THE AMAZING TRANSFORMATIONS OF TOM TERRIFIC

by Kevin Scott Collier

PRESENTED BY

827 North Hollywood Way #100

Burbank, California 91505

Visit us online:

www.cartoonresearch.com

Founder: Jerry Beck

Email: jerrybeck18@gmail.com

INTRODUCTION TO TOM TERRIFIC

By Kevin Scott Collier

I saved the foreword for this book as the final thing to write upon completion of *The Amazing Transformations of Tom Terrific.* I had many great things I wanted to say, but thanks to an elder at our church, he summed it all up for me.

After the Sunday service, my wife and I entered the reception area to chat with fellow congregation members. I approached a man named Jack and engaged in friendly conversation. Knowing I was an author, he enquired, "What new books are you working on?"

I replied, "I've just completed writing a book about *Tom Terrific* with the help of his creator, Gene Deitch. You know who Tom Terrific is, right?"

Jack answered, "Sure." Then he broke out into the *Tom Terrific* theme song, effortlessly breezing through several lines without error.

I struck a huge smile, and thought, *I have the foreword to my book.*

When someone, 60 years after the cartoon first appeared, can sing "I'm Tom Terrific, greatest hero ever," you know Tom was right.

The iconic American humorist Mark Twain once said, "History doesn't repeat itself, but it does rhyme."

It's unlikely there will ever be another character like Tom Terrific, but the melody Gene Deitch created, combining stylistic art, amusing characters, and entertaining stories, will endure forever.

Gene Deitch, aspiring young artist, at age 16.

Gene Deitch draws Tom Terrific for two on his sons, Kim (left) and Simon (right), 1957.

THE ORIGIN OF TOM TERRIFIC

There can be no doubt that Tom Terrific is the greatest hero ever. Why? He tells us so at the beginning of every one of his 26 adventures.

Perhaps the only individual who is greater is Gene Deitch. But he will not tell you that. Others will.

Gene Deitch was born Eugene Merril Deitch on August 8, 1924, to Joseph and Ruth (Delson) Deitch in Chicago, Illinois. His father, a salesman, moved the family to California in 1929.

"As a kid, I was entranced with the idea of cliff-hanger serials," Gene Deitch explained. "At the end of each chapter the hero—or heroine—fallen over the edge of a cliff, was hanging onto a slim branch. And at the bottom of the cliff were several hungry crocodiles. Such a situation of horrendous danger and imminent death was an exciting formula. I carried over this idea in my experimental United Features comic strip, *Terr'ble Thompson*."

But that is getting ahead of the story.

Deitch landed his first professional gig as a cartoonist as a contributor for a jazz magazine in 1941, one year before he graduated from Los Angeles High School.

"I created a series of jazz cartoons, *The Cat*, which presented a single-minded fanatic in an obscure fan magazine, *The Record Changer*," Deitch said. "Any cartoon character hopeful of gaining popularity must be extreme in one way or another, while not being perceived as threatening and seeming to be within acceptable values. All depended on my being in a position of opportunity for practical production."

The Record Changer published *The Cat* from 1941-1951. Deitch also drew cover illustrations and random interior artwork for the periodical.

Gene Deitch cover illustration for *The Record Changer*, featuring *The Cat*, August 1948.

6

The Cat comic by Gene Deitch, published in *The Record Changer* jazz magazine.

Deitch married in 1943. He and his wife, Mary, started a family that numbered three: Kim, Simon and Seth. Growing up with a father who illustrated inspired his boys. All became artists and writers for underground and alternative comics ventures.

During this period, Deitch served in the visual aids department of the training division of Lockheed Aviation Corporation and was a one-time member of the promotional art section of Columbia Broadcasting System, later known as CBS.

Deitch's creative gears had been cranking since childhood. Characters in comic strips that had transitioned successfully to film influenced him.

"For a long time, I was inspired by such diverse comic strips as *Buck Rogers in the 25th Century* and *Krazy Kat*," Deitch explained. "One presented stimulating adventures involving exotic technology and the other explored the concept of diversity. Krazy Kat was threatened by violence, to anything different from the norm, by Ignatz. I needed to limit mindstretching to something simplified enough get produced, positive and entertaining, and different enough from the norms of the time to attract attention."

In 1946, Deitch joined the staff of United Productions of America, an animation studio co-founded by John Hubley. The company originated from the exodus of Disney Studio animators during a 1941 strike. There, Deitch had the opportunity to work with veterans in the cartoon industry.

"By 1956, I had been a fifth wheel with a flat tire at John Hubley's New York branch of his Storyboard Films studio, and not too happy," Deitch recalled. "Due to my ability to draw identifiable, but not too bizarre characters, learned in my career-setting job under the wings of revolutionary animators at UPA, Hub bought my contract, and I was free to take up an offer from New York producer Robert Lawrence, to develop an animation unit within his live-action studio."

Deitch explained that after the short and disappointing stint "with my idol, John Hubley," he was quickly hired as an idea man by Robert Lawrence Productions. No sooner had Deitch settled into Lawrence's Manhattan studio, he met Newt Schwin. Newell T. Schwin, who went by the name

Gene Deitch, 1955, as creative director of United Productions of America, New York studio.

of Newt, was a member of the *Schwinn* bicycle family and an executive at CBS Television's new branch, called CBS Television Film Sales, Inc.

"Newt told me that they had recently purchased the Terrytoons Studio, lock, stock, and barrel full of weird cartoons, from *Farmer Al Falfa* to *Mighty Mouse*," Deitch said. "CBS realized that Terrytoons was probably the worst animation studio in America, but they hungered for any usable cartoon programming."

CBS network logo, 1957.

Terrytoons, tucked away in the town of Rochelle, New York, came with a library that was a landfill of outdated material.

"It was all dated and crappy stuff," Deitch added. "But at that time kids would look at anything that moved or wiggled. Even though old and corn fed, it was new to young kids in the 1950's. It would hold onto the youth market until fresh material could be produced. And that, presumably, is why they went after me. They were offering me the position of creative director of the studio to replace Paul Terry!"

According to Deitch, Terrytoons at the time was the largest animation studio in America, still churning out movie cartoon shorts and insulated from the cartoonist union's decent pay scale. Disney was barely producing animation at the time.

Terrytoons Studio, Rochelle, New York, 1950's.

"We young hotshot UPA types considered it to be the worst animation studio in existence, barely worth a sneer, not having advanced in quality since its silent movie days in the 1920's," Deitch said. "So, why would I want to work in such a place? Well, the reason was, was Newt Schwin. He laid it out to me that Terrytoons was now a wholly-owned CBS unit, needing to be remade in the CBS image, and they somehow believed that I was the man to do it!"

The Columbia Broadcasting System, or CBS, was very familiar with Deitch, as he had worked for them at one time in the 1940's in the promotional art department.

"CBS expected that with me at the creative helm, the Terrytoons studio might actually become viable, and turn out programming up to the CBS standard," Deitch explained. "Based on my UPA/New York reputation, they wanted me to do that for them."

Deitch knew it was the opportunity of a lifetime, but at the same time, he wondered, "How could I just walk out on Bob Lawrence after only a few weeks?" When he approached Robert Lawrence about the Terrytoons offer, the issue saw a civil resolve.

"My first credit in this story goes to Bob Lawrence, who, though disappointed, immediately realized that this was the closest thing to destiny in the life of a cartoonist," Deitch said. "And he gave me his blessing."

There was another slight obstacle to overcome on Deitch's highway to dizzying destiny. It came in the form of Terrytoons business manager William (Bill) Weiss. Schwin informed Deitch that when Paul Terry sold Terrytoons to CBS there was a provision to keep Weiss on for five years.

"Meeting Weiss was like being introduced to a Mafia godfather with a pistol on his lap," Deitch recalls. "He came across as a semi-literate thug, almost bragging about his dubious methods of keeping the animation staff in line, etc., etc. On the way back to Manhattan I sadly told Newt that I could never work for such a man. That's when he told me Terry insisted that Bill Weiss be granted tenure for five years as a condition of the sale."

Deitch decided to take the position as creative director for Terrytoons, even though the Weiss revelation made it clear that he likely wouldn't endure unless he had a similar 5-year guarantee. Deitch marched forward, and Terrytoons was about to receive a major facelift. Hands-on, Deitch scribbled out and created a new Terrytoons logo that animation historians and fans today instantly recognize.

CBS assigned the revived Terrytoons studio the task of creating cartoons for television, which was a new concept. Animation appearing on broadcast television up to that point consisted of older films previously exhibited in movie theaters.

Captain Kangaroo program on CBS, featuring Bob Keeshan as the Captain and Hugh Brannum as Mr. Green Jeans, with Dancing Bear, Mr. Moose, and Bunny Rabbit.

No sooner had Deitch walked into Terrytoons, than the opportunity to create something terrific transpired. What unfolded was *Tom Terrific*, an animated series created for the live-action children's program *Captain Kangaroo*. The character Tom Terrific originated from a syndicated comic strip Deitch created titled *The Real-Great Adventures of Terr'ble Thompson.*

Terr'ble Thompson, a daily comic strip for United Features Syndicate, began publication in newspapers on Sunday, October 16, 1955. Deitch, still working at the animation studios of United Productions of America, hired an assistant, Ruby Davidson, to assist with the strip.

Terr'ble Thompson was a boy who traveled back in time, supporting famous figures to ensure history turned out as recorded in textbooks. The mix included Cleopatra, Napoleon, Nero and Alexander the Great, to name a few. At times these personalities would seek out Terr'ble Thompson at his "World Headquarters," a tree house very similar to Tom Terrific's base of operation.

A few months after the debut of *Terr'ble Thompson*, Deitch was offered the position at Terrytoons, and the strip ceased publication April 14, 1956. Production of the *Tom Terrific* cartoon began later that same year.

The *Tom Terrific* cartoon starred an energetic young boy who wore a thought-proving, funnel-shaped cap. He depended on the lid to think his way in and out of situations where he was needed. A burst of steam from the cone indicated our hero had arrived at a solution.

11

The funnel cap also enabled him to transform himself into anything he pleased. And Tom's amazing transformations allowed him to do almost everything.

Tom's ever-faithful companion, Mighty Manfred the Wonder Dog, was often given credit by selfless Tom for many ingenious solutions. But the truth was that Manfred was more interested in taking naps than in saving the day. The Wonder Dog virtually slept his way through the entire series. Not quite, but Tom's tireless work often contrasted with his faithful friend's bouts with narcolepsy.

Gene Deitch headed up the terrific team behind Tom's cartoon. Bill Weiss served as executive producer. Thomas Morrison conducted busi-

Terr'ble Thompson comic strip by Gene Deitch, 1956.

12

ness as story director. Lionel Wilson was hired to perform every voice for each character in the show.

Among the story writers was Jules Feiffer, who Gene Deitch subsequently worked with on the Oscar-winning animated short *Munro* (1960), and Larz Bourne, whom Deitch called "the great professional gagman."

"Tommy Morrison was actually very helpful to me during my time at Terrytoons," Deitch said. "He was a genuinely good writer, never able to do his best under Terry. We worked well together, and I felt I had his support."

Frank Schudde was appointed production manager on *Tom Terrific*. Animation directors for the series included Connie Rasinski, Dave Tendlar, Mannie Davis, Johnny Gent, Art Bartsch, Ed Donnelly, Manny Davis, Johnny Gentilella, Bob Kuwahara, Vinnie Bell and Tim Tyler, among others.

"Frank 'Sparky' Schudde, the studio production manager, who made everything work, was extremely helpful to me, and outwardly friendly," Deitch recalled.

The veteran animators were talented, but a bit uneasy with creative director Gene Deitch.

Sketches for the creation of the *Tom Terrific* cartoon.

John Tyer (left) and Jules Feiffer (right) worked on the *Tom Terrific* cartoon.

"I always knew that the competent and seemingly sinecure old-timers like Connie Rasinski, Art Bartsch, Ed Donnelly, and Manny Davis, all highly-skilled, but ossified drudges, were unhappy that I had landed on their airstrip, upsetting their comfortable lives," Deitch said.

New blood provided faster circulation in the production, and Deitch had cultivated such a team.

"The marvelously maverick animator Jim Tyer drove full speed onto the highway I was opening up. My 'new gang,' Jules Feiffer, Al Kouzel, Ray Favata, and Eli Bauer, fully backed me," Deitch explained. "Skilled animators Johnny Gentilella, Bob Kuwahara, Vinnie Bell, and others, all helped me."

The budget set for production was small; it wouldn't pay for Manfred's dog food. But Deitch's creativity wasn't just relegated to his storytelling and illustration skills. He used the lack of funds as inspiration to experiment and present something completely foreign to animation. Deitch's staff rose to the occasion.

The characters in the five-minute black and white cliffhangers were all simple, but stylish in execution. All possessed a distinctive character appearance. They were also transparent, void of substance fill. Tom, Manfred, and all guest stars moved over gray washed backgrounds, instead of in front of them. With restricted animation, attention was focused on creating witty dialogue, personalities, and drama that sustained audience attention. The program's background music consisted of a banjo and harmonica.

"Phil Scheib, the long-time, tightly limited composer, who did his best work for me," Deitch said.

Deitch also brought in composer Tod Dockstader and writer Ernest Pinoff on the *Tom Terrific* team.

The first episode of *Tom Terrific* appeared on the *Captain Kangaroo* program June 10, 1957.

Tom Terrific was a notable change for Terrytoons, which had built a reputation on sight gags, rather than upon the strength of writing and characterization. The result was that *Tom Terrific* was enjoyed by children, due to the adventure and the hero's magical transformations, but also by adults, for the gentle satire and episodic formula they had grown up seeing in film serials.

A review published in *Radio Daily-Television Daily* on April 4, 1957, praised the new *Tom Terrific* cartoon.

"*Tom Terrific*, the new *Captain Kangaroo* cartoon character, is the answer to the prayer of any mother who wonders if her children's manners are being too heavily influenced by some cartoon fare on TV," the publication stated. "He is intriguing enough to fulfill a child's requirements for make-believe, and his actions are well within the bounds of good taste. In addition, the current storyline of Tom's attempt to stop Sweet Tooth Sam from stealing candy from children is realistic enough to maintain suspense."

The review also addressed aspects of the production quality and its overall effect for viewers.

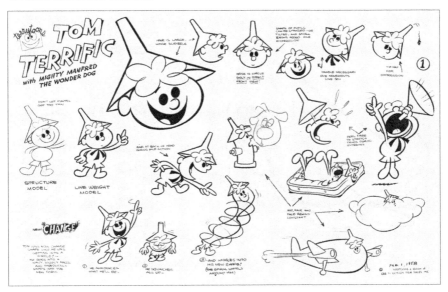

1958 *Tom Terrific* model sheet featuring poses.

"The animation and special effects such as those connected with Tom's thinking are new and refreshing," the periodical continued. "Tom's faithful wonder dog, Manfred — a beast Thurber might have drawn — supplies the necessary comic relief. This cartoon shows fun and excitement without some of the less desirable elements and the gimmicks used to resolve our hero's dilemmas would reward the attention of adult viewers, as well."

Review for *Tom Terrific* reprinted in a Terrytoons promotional advertisement, 1957.

Terrytoons logo created by Gene Deitch.

Terrytoons produced and released two seasons of *Tom Terrific,* which were released in 1957 and 1958. The package included 26 adventure titles in all, evenly divided by year. The last *Tom Terrific* episode appeared on *Captain Kangaroo* on December 15, 1958.

Deitch departed Terrytoons in 1959, moving to Prague, the capital of the Czech Republic. In Prague, he met Zdenka Najmanová, the production manager at the studio where he worked. They married in 1964.

Although his time was brief at Terrytoons, Deitch gained recognition for the company from film critics and at prestigious animation festivals.

The *Tom Terrific* series initially was due to expire its run in September 1961, but remained on *Captain Kangaroo,* due to its popularity, until 1965. At its peak *Tom Terrific* had a viewership of 3.5 million, which still stands as an astounding TV achievement for Terrytoons Studio.

"*Tom Terrific* did become the most successful thing I ever did, but it was after I was out, establishing my own studio, and then off to Prague," Deitch said. "There I produced my Oscar-winning *Munro* cartoon. That had also been originally developed with Jules Feiffer to be produced at Terrytoons, where both Jules and I worked."

Deitch concludes that if *Tom Terrific,* paired with *Munro,* had come out while he worked at Terrytoons, it would have been he who stayed; and it would have convinced the honchos at CBS that they should "assign Weiss to another line of work."

The departure of Gene Deitch from Terrytoons was a creative blow to the company. Until its demise in 1968, Terrytoons pretty much survived due to the talent of animator/director/producer Ralph Bakshi, who quit in 1967. William Weiss resurrected *Mighty Mouse* and *Heckle and Jeckle,* but Terrytoons is best known creatively in the 1960's for Bakshi's *Deputy Dawg* and *The Mighty Heroes.*

A little-known backstory is how *Tom Terrific* was nearly killed-off before it ever aired. While Crabby Appleton, rotten to the core, seems to be the ideal candidate behind the plot, he was not. Tom's greatest threat came from an enemy on the inside.

Don't miss the amazing story, "Tom Terrific's Enemy Within," same channel, same book, next chapter!

Terrytoons founder Paul Terry, who sold Terrytoons to CBS Television in 1956.

TOM TERRIFIC'S ENEMY WITHIN

Tom Terrific creator, Gene Deitch, exited Terrytoons three years after he first walked in the door. It was the beginning of the end for Terrytoons. General manager Bill Weiss gets the credit for the meltdown.

While at Terrytoons Deitch had the full support of CBS, but he still had to deal with Weiss. Deitch approached Newell T. Schwin, asking if it was possible to secure a five-year contract matching the one Paul Terry negotiated for Weiss when he sold the animation studio.

"Newt told me sadly, that could not be done. That they regretted having to grant it to Weiss," Deitch said. "But as insurance, Newt would be assigned as a Terrytoons board member, and would attend every weekly management meeting to protect me against Weiss."

Schwin encouraged Deitch to sweat it out for five years until CBS could dump Weiss.

"What I would need to survive would be to produce at least one hit TV-show to make me fire-proof, before Weiss could nail me for budget overruns on our CinemaScope theater cartoons for 20th Century Fox," Deitch explained. "Creating a modern animation studio out of a moribund one would take experimenting and creative risks, and Weiss, who controlled

18

the accounting department, could easily find ways to keep me over-budget."

But Newt Schwin bailed out after the first season of *Tom Terrific*.

"Schwin, a crackerjack TV show salesman, got an offer he couldn't refuse, and after a lame apology to me, he pedaled off to less poisonous pastures," Deitch said.

Schwin accepted a position as vice president in charge of advertising and public relations with Associates Investment Company of South Bend, Indiana.

No new buffer between Deitch and Weiss was forthcoming.

Terrytoons' Bill Weiss, part of the CBS deal.

"I realized that my Terrytoons days were numbered. My success would be Weiss' doom, and he had to get rid of me well before his contract would expire," Deitch continued. "The first thing he did was to change the venue of the weekly meetings to New York, knowing that I would be too busy to regularly attend. On his part, he never failed to tell the CBS brass how my new style films were going over budget."

New animation methods required experimentation, and new characters in movie cartoons had always needed years to gain popularity. But Deitch wasn't wasting money, he was providing maximum bang for pennies on the dollar.

"The average movie theater viewer might see one, or possibly two, *Clint Clobber* cartoons in a year," Deitch explained, regarding the long-term benefit. "Whereas a short time later, TV cartoon characters were seen once a week, and even daily, and celebrity came quickly. That's audience numbers. That's success."

But the problems with Terrytoons were akin to the tip of the iceberg that sank the Titanic. Nasty things brewing below the surface most crewmen only became aware of much later.

According to *Tom Terrific* story director, Thomas Morrison, in the early days of Terrytoons, Paul Terry had a partner, Frank Moser, whom he wanted to dump so he could gain total ownership.

The narrative precedes that Terry spearheaded a lawsuit against Moser, accusing him of financial finagling. Terry pushed his young accountant, William Weiss, to testify in court against Moser, actually to commit perjury. To buy his silence in any potential countersuit by Moser, Terry promised Weiss a significant share if the studio were ever sold.

"The gangster methods were common in Terrytoons' early years," Deitch explained. "It was a time when film prints were often lowered out the window, away from contesting partners coming with police to claim ownership."

As the story goes, over the years Terry repeated the promise to Weiss, so that he would keep his silence. But Terry secretly made a deal with CBS, allowing him to welch on his promise, by throwing Weiss a 5-year tenure bone.

"No one—not Weiss—not anyone at the studio knew that Terry was, in fact, negotiating to sell the studio to CBS," Deitch recalls. "When it happened, and Terry came into the studio to pick up his personal things, Tommy Morrison, spotted him leaving, and ran up to him."

Apparently, Terry had promised Morrison over the years he would "be taken care of" in the event of a sale. But Morrison read in the morning newspaper that Paul Terry had sold the studio to CBS.

When confronted, Terry reportedly told Morrison "It's none of your [expletive] business!" and walked out, puffing on his cigar. Apparently, Terry didn't share a single cent with any associates left behind, and got himself off the hook with Weiss by insisting, in his sales contract with CBS, that Weiss receive a guaranteed, 5-year tenure.

Morrison, hurt by Terry's exit and broken promises, stayed on and rooted for Deitch during the *Tom Terrific* years. But Deitch knew in the end

The two faces of Bill Weiss chomping on a stogie. One is a photo, the other an illustration by Gene Deitch. Can you guess which one is the cartoon?

that Morrison wouldn't stand up for him and that he was on his way out.

"With the clear realization that a state of war now existed between Weiss and me, I felt that my only hope was for a big success of *Tom Terrific,* now in the final stages of editing," Deitch said. "If *Tom Terrific* would strike gold it would be difficult for Weiss to unseat me. But he had an uncanny instinct for self-preservation, and had spies among several of the old-timers whom he'd convinced that I was planning to fire them."

There were no such intentions by Gene Deitch. He hung on to *Tom Terrific* and placed all his effort into getting the program out, and on the air.

"If a *Tom Terrific* success could then be built on, and I could last until Weiss' mandate ran out, I might survive," Deitch continued. "But Weiss also realized that the cartoon could be a hit. He had to act to pre-empt [it] before *Tom Terrific* was aired."

Weiss prepared the way with propaganda that Deitch was involved in budget overruns. Weiss could manufacture stats, as general manager, and cook the books, making it appear that Deitch could bankrupt the studio.

"All of that went down well enough with the CBS brass, who just didn't want to be bothered with unrest in their insignificant cartoon studio," Deitch said. "All I could do was attempt to cross the finish line before Weiss moved on me. With the departure of Newt Schwin, it gave Weiss the opportunity to convince CBS to nail me before *Tom Terrific* would air."

Frank "Sparky" Schudde, the studio production manager, was in Weiss' office when the bomb dropped on Deitch. Schudde meekly backed his cigar-chomping boss.

"Schudde was clearly brought into the scene specifically for that purpose," Deitch said. "That sealed my fate. I was naively shocked at the betrayal, as he'd given me every indication that he was on my side."

Many of the animators who had worked on *Tom Terrific*, fed up with low-pay and Weiss, departed of their own accord soon after Deitch left.

"It was a tragedy that a bug-eyed monster was able to pull the plug on such a well-positioned outfit, and allow it to go down the drain in a desperate, knee-jerk attempt to save his own scabby skin," Deitch said. "It was just before the technical and marketing revolution that would change everything, but which he could not understand, nor foresee. The death of Terrytoons was Weiss' doing."

Gene Deitch moved on. He left the country and enjoyed a fresh start.

"Another door opened for me, leading to a smaller and more remote garden, a new wife and a new life," he said. "I won my Oscar and grew some nice little flowers, and did well enough financially, but I'll never get over the idea that given a longer chance at Terrytoons, I could have caught the tech tidal wave and surfed into the future Big Time."

But unlike the world of *Tom Terrific*, where innocence and goodness can turn into anything desired, history is immutable. Tom and Manfred were always content no matter the circumstance. Gene Deitch found happiness, but like his time-traveling creations, *Terr'ble Thompson* and *Tom Terrific* knows he made history, too.

"Newt Schwin welched on his promise and left me easy prey to a cigar-smoking predator. But would I have been happier? I doubt it," Deitch concluded. "I'm happy with what I was able to in the following years, kickstarted by the Oscar win just a year later. But that doesn't let Newt Schwin entirely off the hook. I hope he had good luck in his new job."

Newell T. Schwin passed away on June 1, 1977. William Weiss died November 12, 2001.

Terrytoons, during its existence, 1930-1968, received four nominations for Academy Awards, but never won once.

Deitch's *Munro* won an Academy Award for Animated Short Film in 1961. His *Nudnick* cartoon series, released between 1965-1967, with new episodes produced in 1991, received notoriety, too. The pilot episode received a nomination for an Academy Award in 1965.

In 2003, Deitch received the Winsor McCay Award from The International Animated Film Society, ASIFA-Hollywood, for lifetime achievement and contribution to the art of animation.

Munro, Oscar-winning animated short, released in 1960.

TOM TERRIFIC THEME SONGS

The Adventures of Tom Terrific had two different opening theme songs, one for each season. Manfred the Wonder Dog also had a theme song, as well as Tom's nemesis Crabby Appleton, who was rotten to the core. Appleton's song appears in two versions that were presented in the program. Thomas Morrison wrote the lyrics.

TOM OPENING THEME SEASON ONE

Terrytoons presents:
The real, great adventures of me, Tom Terrific!
With Mighty Manfred, the Wonder Dog!
Teeeeeee-Rif-ic!
I'm Tom Terrific, greatest hero ever!
Terrific is the name for me, 'cause I'm so clever.
I can be what I want to be,
and if you'd like to see,
Follow, and follow me!
If you see a plane up-high,
A diesel train go roaring by.
A bumble bee, or a tree, it's me!
When there is trouble,
I'm there on the double.
From Atlantic to Pacific,
They know Tom Terrific!
Aaand, I'm Mighty Manfred, the Wonder dog,
Aaand Tom's ever faithful companion.

TOM OPENING THEME SEASON TWO

Teeeeeee-Rif-ic!
Terrytoons presents:
The real, great adventures of me, Tom Terrific!
With Mighty Manfred, the Wonder Dog!
I'm Tom Terrific, great adventure lover!
With Mighty Manfred at my side, villains run for cover.
I can be anything you see, change my shape most readily,
How I do it puzzles me!
If you see a rocket blast,
A sailing ship come sailing past.
A little flea, a golden key, it's me!

23

All kinds of fun things,
I'm never just one thing.
T-E-R-R-ific,
My name's Tom Terrific!
Aaand, I'm Mighty Manfred, the Wonder dog,
Aaand Tom's ever faithful companion.

MANFRED THE WONDER DOG THEME SONG

I'm Mighty Manfred (uh) the Wonder Dog.
Noble strain, able brain, that's me.
Fast and fleet of feet, danger is my meat,
I'm fearless, brave as any hound can be.
I'm Mighty Manfred (uh) the Wonder Dog.
Tried and true, handsome too, this I know.
There's just no dog like me,
It's true because you see,
Tom Terrific told me so.

CRABBY APPLETON THEME VERSION I

My name is Crabby Appleton,
and I am simply awful.
It does my heart a lot of good
to do a deed unlawful!
I'm fond of gloom, impending doom,
I think good deeds are sappy!
I laugh with glee, it pleases me
when everyone's unhappy.

CRABBY APPLETON THEME VERSION 2

My name is Crabby Appleton,
I'm rotten to the core.
I do a bad deed every day,
and sometimes three or four.
I can't stand fun for anyone,
I think good deeds are sappy,
I laugh with glee, it pleases me,
when everyone's unhappy.

There is one more theme song in the series, "Pittsburgh the Pirate," which appears in "Robinsnest Crusoe."

Lionel Wilson
ALL VOICES
ON

Thanks
GENE DEITCH
TOM MORRISON

TERRYTOONS'

NEW ADVENTURE CARTOON SERIES

TOM TERRIFIC

TO BE RELEASED SOON ON "CAPTAIN KANGAROO"
OVER THE CBS TELEVISION NETWORK

© 1956 — TERRYTOONS, A DIVISION OF CBS TELEVISION FILM SALES, INC.

Terrytoons advertisement promoting Lionel Wilson as all of the voices behind the upcoming *Tom Terrific* television cartoon.

25

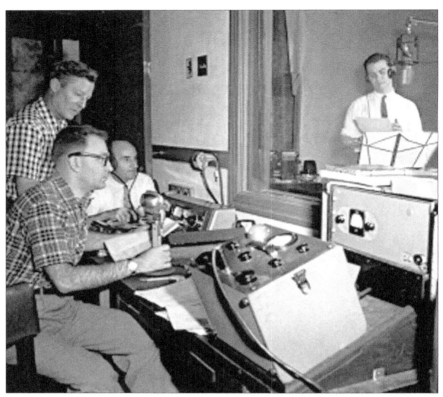

Lionel Wilson (in the recording booth at right) prepares to read from a *Tom Terrific* script. Gene Deitch (front, left) and Tommy Morrison (standing) in the recording studio.

THE TERRIFIC VOICE

Lionel Wilson bears the distinction of being all of the voices appearing in the *Tom Terrific* cartoon. The *TV Radio Mirror* magazine made the general public aware of this in its July 1957 issue.

"In the new CBS-TV Terrytoons series, *Tom Terrific*, Lionel does every voice you hear," the magazine reported. "Nearly fifty-two in all."

Born Lionel Lazarus Salzer on March 22, 1924, in Brooklyn, New York, Wilson was less than five months older than Gene Deitch when work commenced on *Tom Terrific*.

The son of Jonas and Sylvia Salzer, his father, a Lithuania immigrant, received a doctorate and provided for the family as a chemist for the Edelbrew Brewery Company in Brooklyn.

Salzer developed an interest in acting while attending Erasmus High School in Brooklyn. There he changed his name to Lionel Wilson for professional purposes.

After graduation Wilson earned a theater scholarship for his acting achievement. While drama club provided a practice platform, Wilson credited a neighbor with helping shape his talent, arrange auditions and find him work.

"I got a lucky start as a star," Wilson told *TV Radio Mirror* magazine. "It was my luck that our neighbor in Brooklyn was a professional acting coach. She took me in hand and made my career."

Wilson began his career in the late 1940's with NBC radio in bit roles. One notable appearance was on the suspense espionage radio show *Top Secret,* starring Ilona Massey. In the episode, Wilson played a private eye. During the program, he delivered a perfect imitation of Massey's sultry sex-tones, without the audience knowing it was he.

Wilson began his television career in 1949 on *The Aldrich Family* TV series, in the role of George Bigalow. He also appeared in *Armstrong Cir-*

BROOKLYN EAGLE, SUNDAY, JUNE 7, 1942

WIN STAGE HONORS—Lionel Wilson, 18, a recent graduate of Erasmus Hall High School, was selected as one of the winners of scholarships in the Barter Theater, Abingdon, Va. Left to right are Mildred Notwick, judge for the award; Mr. Wilson and Margaret Phillips, who also was given a scholarship.

Lionel Wilson (center) in a *Brooklyn Eagle* article published June 7, 1942.

cle Theater in the episode "Jackpot."

Subsequently Wilson starred in several Broadway plays and acted in *Valiant Lady, Search for Tomorrow,* and a string of other top episodic, dramatic daytime shows.

He counted among his friends actors Jimmy Kirkwood, Kathy McGuire and Dolores Sutton.

At the time he was recording voices for *Tom Terrific*, Wilson, single, resided in an apartment in Manhattan, New York. He found more work behind the camera than in front of one delivering voices for TV. Thus, Wilson primarily made a name for himself doing voice overs.

Lionel Wilson (at left) during the making of *Tom Terrific*.

"Lionel is up to a hundred different voices on the air," *TV Radio Mirror* reported. "On toothpaste ads, for example, he is both villain (Mr. Decay) and the hero (Mr. Toothpaste). He's both rabbits for a laundry starch and a couple of million other things for other commercials."

After *Tom Terrific*, Lionel Wilson was the voice of many subsequent Terrytoons cartoons, such as *Sidney the Elephant* and *Stanley the Lion*. Wilson also did the voice of Ropeman, Cuckoo Man and most of the villains in Ralph Bakshi's superhero team parody *The Mighty Heroes*.

At the age of 75, in 1999, Wilson landed the role of Eustace Bagge on the Cartoon Network animated series *Courage the Cowardly Dog*.

After 33 episodes as Eustace, Wilson retired due to illness. He died of pneumonia on April 30, 2003, at the age of 79.

Sixty years after the program originated, the voices in *Tom Terrific* are alive and well thanks to the talent of Lionel Wilson.

THE NASTY KNIGHT

(Season 1, Episode 1 / First Broadcast June 10, 1957)

Tom Terrific decides to become a tree in King Arthur's courtyard, transporting he and Manfred the Wonder Dog back in time. Once there, the pair notice tears falling from a castle tower. They go to investigate.

Tom discovers a sobbing princess consoled by her father, the king. The fair young maiden wishes to be wed to her one true love, Feeble Fred, but it doesn't seem possible. Fred must defeat the armored juggernaut Sir Nasty Knight in battle in the arena to win her hand in marriage.

Tom Terrific decides he must intervene. But upon meeting Feeble Fred, who cannot even bear to wear his armor because it makes him itch, Tom realizes this will be a real challenge. When he encounters Sir Nasty Knight before the match Tom finds out how he got the name "Nasty."

Feeble Fred is in the arena, sans armor or weapon. Tom joins him to help out and promises not to cheat. "I must never take unfair advantage of anyone," he says.

The battle for the hand of the princess commences. After running some transformation interference, Tom Terrific evens the playing field - making it a fair fight - by turning into a magnet and stripping Sir Nasty Knight of his armor. As a result, the unarmed villain pleads for his life and relinquishes the contest for the princess to Fred. Thus, the princess can wed her true love.

THE PILL OF SMARTNESS

(Season 1, Episode 2 / First Broadcast June 17, 1957)

While watching a TV program, Tom Terrific and Manfred the Wonder Dog learn about the Pill of Smartness. It is hidden in the Sphinx in Egypt, and whosoever discovers it will experience great wisdom. Thus, Tom transforms into an Egyptian chariot to fly them there.

Tom Terrific discovers Crabby Appleton is at the Sphinx, no doubt in search of the pill for evil purposes. Appleton uses several clever ruses to throw off their search for the pill.

Tom is tricked into navigating a tunnel and becomes trapped inside a room. After transforming into a bone, Manfred finds and rescues Tom.

Crabby Appleton hypnotizes Manfred into thinking he's a mouse and Tom a piece of cheese. The dog gives chase, but the distraction ends when Tom snaps his companion out of the trance.

Tom and Manfred spot the Pill of Smartness in the hand of a statue of Cleopatra. It appears Appleton has outwitted the duo when Manfred falls from the statue. Tom transforms into a rope to catch him, tying the two up. However, when Appleton beats them to the punch and swallows the pill, he doesn't gain wisdom but displays the behavior of a baby.

Reading hieroglyphics in the Sphinx, Tom discovers the pill doesn't work for those with evil intentions. He concludes the key to becoming smarter isn't a pill but achieved by study and learning more at school.

SWEET TOOTH SAM

(Season 1, Episode 3 / First Broadcast June 24, 1957)

It's raining empty candy boxes from the sky. Tom Terrific and Manfred the Wonder Dog look up and spy Sweet Tooth Sam in an airplane dropping candy wrappers. They discover he's on a mission to steal candy away from all the children on Earth.

Tom and Manfred arrive in the town of Nut Cluster to find children in tears. Tom assures them he will restore things. But when confronting Sweet Tooth Sam, it results in the pair hanging onto the edge of a cliff. After escaping the dilemma, Tom and Manfred track Sam to his cabin, where Tom turns into a magnifying glass that heats the bullets on Sam's gun belt, blasting a hole in which the bandit falls. Tom and Manfred recover the stolen candy and place it in a bag, but the candy bandit blows it up.

While Sam uses an abandoned mine to melt down stolen candy, Tom and Manfred discover the cave and are captured. Sam places them in a cauldron of melted chocolate which turns the pair into a huge candy bar. Manfred eats the bar from the inside, allowing their freedom.

In the end, the cave collapses. The town of Nut Cluster above falls into the open space, which propels the candy inside skyward. It then rains down on the cheering children. Sam loses his sweet tooth and no longer has a taste for sweets.

SNOWY PICTURE
(Season 1, Episode 4 / First Broadcast July 1, 1957)

While going through fan mail from children who watch his TV show, Tom Terrific discovers a letter from an Eskimo at the North Pole saying they are having problems receiving the program. The weak reception has given them a snowy picture.

Tom Terrific and Manfred the Wonder Dog travel to the North Pole, where they find their Eskimo fans. After receiving a gift of strawberry popsicles, Tom enters an igloo to examine a television set. The inhabitants are receiving local channels just fine, but transmission of Tom's program from the tower atop the Empire State Building isn't getting through.

Nighttime has begun at the pole, and it lasts six months. Tom, navigating in darkness, finds Manfred in a cave sleeping with hibernating polar bears. After waking an angry bear, and with some coaxing, Tom changes into a cat to wake Manfred and motivate him to give chase. Manfred isn't too pleased with the trick, but joins Tom on the mission.

Arriving in New York, via Tom's transformation into a sports car of which Manfred is at the wheel, they are stopped by a police officer. He's about to arrest the pooch until Tom appears and explains their mission. He turns into an elevator to bring them to the top of the Empire State Building, where they fix the television transmission tower, bringing joy to their Eskimo fans who can now watch their TV program.

CRABBY APPLETON'S DRAGON

(Season 1, Episode 5 / First Broadcast July 8, 1957)

Tom Terrific and Manfred the Wonder Dog are on the ocean in a rowboat looking for treasure. A giant wave washes Manfred overboard, sending him to the ocean bottom where he finds an enormous oyster. Tom joins him, sees the oyster, and believes the creature is in pain. He turns into a pepper shaker, causing the crustacean to sneeze and expel the pearl.

Returning to the boat with the pearl, Tom tells Manfred he plans to donate the value of the pearl to the House for Homeless hounds. But Crabby Appleton, in a mini-sub, spies the pearl using a periscope. He wants it to buy a furnace that will melt all the ice cream on the planet.

Back inside his island lair, Appleton inflates a giant, floating rubber sea dragon to scare Tom and Manfred and take the pearl. Tom drains the water level and beaches the dragon upon a rock, but safety runs out when Appleton inflates the rubber hazard to an enormous size and sends it their way.

Manfred the Wonder Dog's tail punctures a hole in the dragon, sending it sailing off over the horizon, and casting the pearl into Appleton's possession. Tom sneaks into Appleton's lair and turns into the madman's controller machine in his absence. When Appleton returns, Tom takes control and revives the dragon, which carries Appleton away. The pearl returns to the heroic duo.

CAPTAIN KIDNEY BEAN
(Season 1, Episode 6 / First Broadcast July 15, 1957)

Seeking adventure, Tom Terrific transports himself, with Manfred the Wonder Dog, back in time, to the days of pirates on the high seas. The pair meets pirate Captain Kidney Bean outside an inn and discovers him stealing a chest full of coins. The rotten pirate has taken the community treasure chest reserved for sick, old sailors.

Manfred ends up inside a sack, unnoticed, in the captain's wagon, and is taken by the pirate to his ship. Tom follows, hot on their trail. His mission: to retrieve his faithful pal and return the treasure chest to its rightful owners.

Falling through a trap door into Kidney Bean's cavern hide-out, Tom finds Manfred tied up, and is taken a prisoner, too. Tom escapes and boards the captain's ship to rescue Manfred. The crew place Tom in a chest and toss him overboard into the sea.

After escaping the situation, Tom is back at the sailing pirate ship. Knocked back into the sea, Tom sees Manfred and crew at the ship's railing. It appears Manfred has become a pirate, too. Tom realizes it must be a trick and transforms into a ship in pursuit. He's rejoined with Manfred, but the pirates have gone to Bloodshot Island to bury the treasure.

Arriving at the island, Tom turns into a Geiger counter, finds the treasure, and returns it to its owners to benefit the sick, old sailors.

THE GRAVITY MAKER

(Season 1, Episode 7 / First Broadcast July 22, 1957)

Tom Terrific discovers Manfred is off accepting a cushy position for a dog at the Ivory Tower. The job requires nothing and offers plenty to eat. Thus, Tom heads to the Ivory Tower in search of his faithful companion.

The Ivory Tower is the lair of Isotope Feeney, a scientific meanie. He welcomes the dog, accepting him as his "employee." Tom arrives at the tower and begs Manfred to come home, to no avail. Feeney takes Manfred up into the tower. His plan is to use Manfred in anti-gravity experiments.

Tom turns into a bee and flies up into the tower, where he finds Feeney using a TV camera-like device that elevates Manfred from a couch to the ceiling. After bringing the dog back down, Feeney uses the device to raise a mailbox outdoors. Feeney relishes his newfound power and cherishes the gravity of the situation.

Feeney sprays Tom with a Happy Mist, which makes him believe he is a real bee. Tom journeys outdoors to work, flying between flowers and a hive to make honey.

Tom snaps out of it and finds Manfred nearby seated on a stump, with Feeney pointing his device at the dog. But Manfred keeps falling off the stump and out of the anti-gravity beam. Feeney finds himself in the beam and is stuck up in a tree.

Feeney is released after he promises not to tinker with gravity again.

SCRAMBLED DINOSAUR EGGS

(Season 1, Episode 8 / First Broadcast July 29, 1957)

While visiting the Museum of Natural History, Manfred the Wonder Dog topples a dinosaur skeleton when attracted to acquiring the biggest (dog) bone in the world. Reassembling the frame produces no remedy. So Tom and Manfred go back in time to correct the problem.

Tom transforms into a dinosaur nest, but no mother dinosaur takes the bait. Tom and Manfred chance upon an Allosaur and several other species. Manfred takes a ride on the back of a Brontosaurus and ends up stuck on a cliff. Tom mistakes Manfred's nose as a dinosaur egg. Manfred also takes a ride aloft on a Rhamphorhynchus who drops him into her nest of babies on a mountainside.

Tom Terrific comes to his rescue and the two fall into a river below. Tom, atop the buoyant dog, paddles his way and the pair are soon atop a Plesiosaur zipping through the water. But the imminent danger is a volcano about to erupt. Tom transforms into a hot air balloon to carry he and his faithful companion to safety, returning them to the present day at the Museum of Natural History.

Once there, they discover what was believed to be a rock that had fallen into the basket of the air balloon is a dinosaur egg, which hatches before their eyes. To their surprise, the museum workers had fixed the skeleton during their absence and momma dinosaur appears to retrieve her baby.

WHO STOLE THE NORTH POLE?
(Season 1, Episode 9 / First Broadcast August 6, 1957)

Tom Terrific and Manfred the Wonder Dog hear a boat whistle and discover a lost ocean liner navigating a corn field. A boy scout passes by whose compass doesn't work. When Santa Claus appears at their headquarters, he tells them someone has stolen the North Pole.

Tom turns into a pelican and asks a formation of geese where they are heading. When he learns they travel south, he knows north is in the opposite direction. Tom transforms into an airplane to bring he and Manfred to the North Pole.

Their suspicion as to the culprit behind the missing pole proves to be correct. It's Crabby Appleton. And he has plans to steal the South Pole, too. Tom and Manfred journey to Echo Canyon, a trap set by Appleton. He triggers an avalanche. To avoid being crushed, Tom turns into an igloo.

Appleton captures Manfred and puts him to use as his sled dog to make his escape. Tom turns into a rolling snowball in hot pursuit. He catches up to the evil one and knocks him from the sled.

Tom discovers Appleton has sliced the pole into pieces and sold them around the world as souvenirs. Tom threatens to tell Santa of his deed unless he recovers every part. Appleton complies and the pole is restored.

Satisfied with the result, Santa gives Appleton a gift. A gag gift. It's a jack-in-the-box bearing a likeness of Crabby's head.

INSTANT TANTRUMS
(Season 1, Episode 10 / First Broadcast August 13, 1957)

Tom Terrific and Manfred the Wonder Dog both find themselves up trees as a result of Mr. Instant, who is behind the feat. Mr. Instant, using a secret formula powder, can make anything instantly. He warns the two his latest invention, Instant Tantrum powder, will be used to stop children from being happy.

After getting out of the trees, Tom and Manfred discover a previously happy child having a tantrum. Mr. Instant tries to blow a cloud of tantrum powder in Tom's direction, but our hero blows back. The cloud returns and effects Manfred. Tom changes into a bucket of water tossed upon his faithful companion to snap him out of it.

Tom and Manfred trail Mr. Instant back to his secret laboratory. There, the villain creates an instant kite, sending Manfred aloft. Around the dog's neck is a box of Tantrum Powder to be released via a storm cloud raining down on the town below. Tom transforms into a weather dial to stop the threat, but breaks. He then turns into an umbrella to shield the kite, powder, and Manfred from the rain.

Mr. Instant escapes back to his lab, where he readies a missile to shoot the powder over the town. When rain soaks the villain, all his Instant Powder is activated, burying him in a pile of items. He throws a tantrum and destroys everything in his lab. Thus, problem solved in an instant.

TRACK MEET, WELL DONE

(Season 1, Episode 11 / First Broadcast August 20, 1957)

Tom Terrific and Manfred the Wonder Dog watch kids play baseball. A boy named Paul Puny approaches them. The weakling is not allowed to join the game. Tom assures Paul strength is not required, but confidence.

Tom brings the boy to talk to team manager Musclehead. But the bully won't allow the Paul or his puny friends to join. Musclehead flees after a transformation confrontation with Tom.

Tom believes he has made matters worse. Manfred suggests a track meet. Tom assembles the boys and assures them, "Lots of great athletes are little."

Tom confronts Musclehead at the gymnasium and gets stuffed into and trapped inside, a gym locker. The track meet goes on, but the puny kids are no match for Musclehead. Manfred retrieves Tom, but it's too late. The bully has defeated his little, weak opponents.

Tom feels he has let the kids down. He comes up with the idea of giving each child a pair of magic shoes, which can enable one to run faster and jump higher than anyone else. It appears to work, as the kids crush Musclehead and his gang in all the events. But the shoes are nothing special. Confidence allows the boys to win and the kids discover that.

At the conclusion, Musclehead invites the children to play on his baseball team. Confidence wins!

THE GREAT CALENDAR MYSTERY

(Season 1, Episode 12 / First Broadcast August 27, 1957)

Tom Terrific and Manfred the Wonder Dog travel to Nathaniel Annual's Calendar Factory to pay a visit.

Nathaniel gives them a tour of the Holiday Department, where they see an enormous machine known as the holiday distributor. It is responsible for the placement of special days on the yearly calendar. It also places Saturdays and Sundays, important to kids, too, as being the days they are not required to attend school.

While strolling about, Tom and Manfred discover Nathaniel Annual has hired Crabby Appleton to be his assistant. Annual puts Appleton in charge of the holiday distributor machine. It proves to be a mistake, as Appleton's plans are to keep all the holidays, and Saturdays and Sundays, for himself.

It's only after departing Nathaniel Annual's Calendar Factory that Tom discovers what Appleton achieved. The calendars everyone is using are missing all holidays and days off.

Appleton journeys into the Dandyland Amusement Park. Because of the revised calendar he has the place all to himself.

Tom spies Appleton in Dandyland and causes it to rain, ruining his fun. He tells the villain he'll stop the rain if he returns the weekends and holidays to the calendar.

Appleton complies. Weekends and holidays are for all to enjoy again.

ELEPHANTS STEW

(Season 1, Episode 13 / First Broadcast September 3, 1957)

Tom Terrific and Manfred the Wonder Dog journey to Africa for adventure. Tom turns into a rocket ship to transport them there.

Upon arrival, they witness stampeding animals and discover the cause, a lion, who is king of the jungle. But he presents no danger. He's shy and bashful. The lion tells Tom and Manfred it is not he whom others fear, but a mad elephant. Tom assures the lion he will be restored as king of the jungle and the elephant will be addressed.

Tom and Manfred face several obstacles on the way to finding the elephant, including traversing a river full of crocodiles and a hippopotamus.

Confronting the pachyderm, Tom gets a first-hand experience of the beast's anger when it tosses him through the air. Tom decides to fight fear with fear and transforms into a mouse to scare the creature. It works, and the elephant now experiences what it is like to be frightened.

Tom and Manfred learn the beast is angry with himself. Elephants are not supposed to forget, but he has. He buried a stash of special peanuts in a safe and cannot recall where he put them. Tom helps by explaining that anger causes forgetfulness. Thus, the elephant calms and remembers the location and combination of the safe.

The elephant finds peace and happiness, and the lion reassumes his role as King of the jungle.

THE MISSING MAIL MYSTERY

(Season 2, Episode 1 / First Broadcast September 22, 1958)

Tom Terrific expresses concern when mail from his fans doesn't arrive. He asks the postman to double-check his bag, but finds nothing. Tom figures his pen pals must all be sick.

Tom changes into a mail plane and travels around the globe. He discovers children are not ill and are sending him plenty of letters.

Tom Terrific becomes a postage stamp to put himself through the mail and see where the problem is. Attaching himself to a pen pal's letter in Rome, Manfred slides Tom into a mailbox. Crabby Appleton grabs the letter from the box.

Back at Appleton's hideout, Crabby steams Tom off the envelope and places him in his stamp collector's album. He has stolen the hero's letters for the stamps, and now has a rare collection representing nations around the world. Tom is rendered helpless, stuck in the album.

Tom changes into a dog bone to attract Manfred to his location. Manfred licks him free. Tom travels to the North pole where an Eskimo girl assists Tom with a plan, applying whale blubber glue to stamps.

Appleton steals the letter, but the stamps don't make it into his album. They become permanently affixed to his tongue. Appleton appeals to Tom for the antidote to the glue. He promises Tom he won't tamper with his mail anymore. Thus, the missing letter mystery is stamped out.

THE PRINCE FROG

(Season 2, Episode 2 / First Broadcast September 29, 1958)

Tom Terrific is reading Manfred the Wonder Dog a book of fairy tales and imagines they should visit fairyland. They arrive and see a wondrous land of peppermint trees and lemonade waterfalls. They also see a crying prince.

Tom introduces he and Manfred to the enchanted prince, and discovers he is the recipient of a witch's spell. He once was a happy frog. The spell turned him into a very unhappy prince, but he desires to return to his former amphibian self, and reunite with his friends and life in the pond.

Tom and Manfred go in search of the witch to persuade her to reverse the spell. On their way, they encounter Jack-be-nimble and Humpty Dumpty. Arriving at a cabin, Witch One invites the pair inside.

Witch One seeks to help. She looks up a solution in a book of how to undo evil spells to reverse the curse. She lists several things that must be found and assembled to break the spell. Tom and Manfred set off to acquire every ingredient. They secure a pebble from a peak, pepper from the beanstalk giant, and a blade of grass from the Black Forest.

Tom and Manfred give the witch the ingredients and once combined, she can change the prince back into his happy, hopping self.

Witch One also momentarily changes Manfred into a rabbit, and back, just for fun.

ISOTOPE FEENY'S FOOLISH FOG

(Season 2, Episode 3 / First Broadcast October 6, 1958)

Tom Terrific notices Isotope Feeny's Ivory Tower aglow after 8 o'clock in the evening, meaning he must be conducting experiments.

Feeny is developing his latest invention, Feeny's Foolish Fog, that can turn the most intelligent person into a nincompoop. He places all the ingredients into his foolish fog simulator.

When Tom wakes in the morning, he spies puffs of polka-dot smoke in the sky, coming from the Ivory Tower, heading in his direction.

Feeny's Foolish Fog effects Manfred and the dog goes bonkers. Manfred snaps out of it and Tom concludes it is a foolish fog.

Suddenly, the wind changed direction, and the polka-dot puffs of smoke move to the city. But if Tom ends up in the mist he will act foolishly too, and be unable to rescue the townsfolk.

Tom imagines if he is invisible the fog cannot affect him. Thus, he changes into an invisible racing car to transport he and Manfred quickly to the city.

They arrive too late. The fog has made everyone a fool. Tom and Manfred head to the Ivory Tower to stop Isotope Feeny, who is preparing to unleash enough fog to cover the world.

Tom turns into a fan and blows the fog back at Feeny, rendering him foolish and no longer a threat to society.

MOON OVER MANFRED

(Season 2, Episode 4 / First Broadcast October 13, 1958)

Tom Terrific peers out his treehouse window and discovers the moon has lost its glow and gone dark. What went wrong? Tom turns into a rocket ship to transport he and Manfred the Wonder Dog to the moon to investigate the crisis.

The rocket ship veers off course, goes down a chimney, and into the basement of an apartment building. Tom and Manfred momentarily believe they are on the moon. But when an elevator deposits them outside the duo see they are still on Earth.

Tom becomes a radio wave and transports he and Manfred to the moon. There they meet the Man in the Moon, who is preparing to leave. Since humankind began sending satellites into space the sky over the moon are beeping with activity. He plans to relocate to a quieter planet.

He shows Tom the dials to control the moon's phases and brightness, leaving it in his hands, then departs. Tom turns into a meteor and enters space to find a replacement, but is unable to break free of the moon's gravity. When all seems lost, Manfred moves the dials and disrupts the moon, prompting the Man in the Moon's return.

The man knows he cannot leave the management of the moon to amateurs. Tom inspires him to value his job because so many on Earth appreciate all he does. Tom and Manfred return to Earth on a moonbeam.

GO WEST, YOUNG MANFRED

(Season 2, Episode 5 / First Broadcast October 20, 1958)

Tom Terrific and Manfred the Wonder Dog head west for adventure, but initially wind up in present day California. Tom turns into a clock that ticks backward and transports them to the days of the great gold rush.

There, Tom and Manfred witness a wagon train under attack by Indians in the distance. Addressing the desperate situation, Tom turns into a bugle and sounds a charge, tricking the Indians into fleeing because they believe the Calvary is on the way. It saves a pioneer, thanks to Tom.

Manfred assists in their journey to California, pulling the wagon with Tom and the pioneer. When they arrive at the gateway to the west, they encounter a checkpoint. They must pay a toll to allow passage. The fee is one bag of gold. Thus, Tom pans for gold in a nearby stream, securing passage. He turns into a saddlebag to hold the gold nuggets, and he and Manfred hitch a ride with the Pony Express back to the toll booth.

They encounter Indians on the way. Manfred falls off a horse and ends up in the Indian settlement. Manfred's native-like dance, a result of cactus needles stuck in his behind from the fall, has the Indians welcoming him with open arms. They make him an honorary chief.

Tom is alarmed when he realizes Manfred is missing, and he and the pioneer go to his rescue. They discover he has befriended the people. Tom persuades Manfred to rejoin him, and Manfred bids the tribe farewell.

THE SILLY SANDMAN
(Season 2, Episode 6 / First Broadcast October 27, 1958)

Mighty Manfred the Wonder Dog arrives at Tom Terrific's tree house with a string of cans tied to his tail. Manfred and Tom head to town and discover naughty children pranksters. Kids everywhere seem to be cranky and irritable. The reason is a lack of sleep.

Something has happened to The Sandman, who fails to come at night. Children are not receiving his wondrous dream dust anymore. Tom and Manfred head to the Sierra Desert, a bastion of sand, to locate The Sandman. They find his tent at the Greenland Oasis, but he is not there.

The pair travel to Switzerland where they locate The Sandman atop the Matterhorn. Tom turns into a yodel and summons the master of sleep back to the Oasis, but he will not budge. Tom turns into a steam cloud to lift he and Manfred to the top of the Matterhorn.

They encounter The Sandman sledding, having fun in the snow. Tom explains the sleepless dilemma, but The Sandman is reluctant to go back to his purpose. He's enjoyed playing in daylight and is not ready to resume his twilight night-shift job. Tom explains that with the sun and the Earth's rotation, and it's both daytime and nighttime for half the globe.

The issue resolved, The Sandman will spread dream dust where it is dark, then head off to play in areas of daylight. Repeating the pattern returns the children to sweet dreams.

CRABBY PARK

(Season 2, Episode 7 / First Broadcast November 4, 1958)

Tom Terrific and Manfred the Wonder Dog are alarmed when they discover all the trees have disappeared, including the one that supported their tree house.

The oddity has affected everyone. The Forest Ranger is out of a job. Kids have no place to hang swings or play hide and seek. Woodpeckers are out of luck. The tree surgeon must find new patients. Birds have nowhere to nest, so a bird creates a home atop Manfred's head.

Tom suspects Crabby Appleton is behind the forestry theft. He turns into a tree for the villain to steal. It works, and Tom and Manfred discover that Crabby has taken the trees to create his very own, private park.

While inside Crabby's Park, Tom and Manfred become separated. Tom goes in search of his trusty companion, but Appleton tricks Tom concerning direction to confuse him, and he becomes lost. Manfred runs into Crabby, who informs him "no dogs are allowed" in his park.

Tom becomes a butterfly and travels over the trees. He finds Manfred and the two are reunited. Manfred walks off a cliff, ending up in the river below, headed for a waterfall. Tom rescues him.

To close Crabby's Park, Tom becomes a calendar and changes the season to fall. With millions of leaves coming off the trees, Crabby has no desire to rake them all up. Thus, every tree is returned to its proper place.

THE MILLION MANFRED MYSTERY

(Season 2, Episode 8 / First Broadcast November 11, 1958)

Tom Terrific runs an errand to the store and leaves Manfred the Wonder Dog behind at the tree house. He also leaves behind his funnel cap, which Manfred put on his head.

A flying saucer lands atop the tree house and three tiny Martians step out. They enter Tom's headquarters where they find Manfred asleep. Examining the dog, they create a replica of Manfred using modeling clay. The aliens then abduct Manfred, taking him into, and away, in their saucer, leaving the model behind.

Tom returns, recovers his cap, and discovers the clay likeness of Manfred. Suddenly a million flying saucers land on earth, each releasing replicas of Manfred. They quickly infiltrate cities and homes.

Tom commandeers a saucer, taking it to Mars. There he sees the replica factory turning Martians into Manfreds. Tom returns to Earth, knowing that among the countless Wonder Dogs on our planet, one is the real deal.

Tom searches to no avail. He returns to the tree house and finds the real Manfred and a Martian he has befriended. Truth be told, the Martians wanted to appear to Earthlings as Tom, so humanity would not fear, but love them. Manfred, wearing Tom's cap, created the misunderstanding.

With no hard feelings, the visitors depart with an open invitation to return anytime.

THE FLYING SORCERER
(Season 2, Episode 9 / First Broadcast November 18, 1958)

Tom Terrific and Manfred the Wonder Dog travel back to ancient Bagdad to the days of sorcery and magic.

There they encounter a giant genie in tears. The sad, gentle gargantuan explains that he cannot return to his magic lamp because the last person who possessed it failed to use all three wishes. And he cannot remember who his last master was. Until the third wish occurs, he's out in the cold.

Tom and Manfred seek a solution from The Flying Sorcerer. He offers a riddle that will reveal the answer. So Tom and Manfred head off, following the clues in the rhyme. Tom turns into a dish and catches a fish in the lake, meeting part of the riddle's demands. Manfred drinks all the water, which is cherry flavored, meeting another requirement.

The pair meets Sinbad the Sailor, who is gathering fish from the dry lake bed in a pail. He mentions he's yet to uses his "third wish," then vanishes. Tom and Manfred are on his trail. They follow the final riddle clue and run into Ali Baba. He provides a passageway through a mountain so they can continue their hunt.

Tom and Manfred find Sindbad atop a mountain of fish. Manfred eats the fish, bringing Sinbad to ground level. He is so mad about losing his catch that he wishes Tom and Manfred would disappear.

Thus, the third wish is made, and the genie happily returns to his lamp.

THE BIG DOG SHOW-OFF

(Season 2, Episode 10 / First Broadcast November 25, 1958)

Tom Terrific decides to enter Manfred the Wonder Dog in The Big Dog Show. Crabby Appleton is at the event, in hiding, and up to no good.

Unseen, Appleton tricks Manfred into swallowing a helium-filled balloon that resembles a sausage, sending the dog aloft. Up, up and away, Appleton thinks. But Manfred descends back into the event. Appleton's dog enters the competition, but no one knows that who the owner is.

Tom changes into a cat to show the judge how active Manfred is. Every dog at the show gives chase, but Manfred, who sleeps through it. The judge awards Manfred points for being the only dog that not to chase the cat. Good behavior, mind you.

Tom turns into a spotlight to highlight sleeping Manfred, who wakes to perform his "Manfred song." However, the judge doesn't see it, as his hat covered his eyes. Appleton's dog performs for the judge and it appears he's won the contest. Manfred then becomes draped in a blanket and carries out a silly dance, which impresses the judge

However, both Manfred and Appleton's dogs are disqualified. Manfred is booted because "no talking dogs" are allowed in this show. Appleton is out, too. He never had a dog—it was really Crabby inside a dog costume.

In conclusion, Manfred's prize is a first class dog bone, given to him by the one who knows he's a winner—Tom Terrific.

THE END OF RAINBOWS
(Season 2, Episode 11 / First Broadcast December 1, 1958)

After a rain shower, Tom Terrific and Manfred the Wonder Dog journey on a rainbow to find what is at the end. But they are alarmed when they discover the end is incomplete. Landing in Rainbow County, the pair encounters the artist, Mr. Rembrandt, has run out of color.

Tom and Manfred volunteer to help, guaranteeing they can find all the colors to refill his large paint pots. But there is little time. The duo has to deliver all of the colors before the next rain, or there will be no rainbow.

They journey to Yellowstone, Wyoming, to secure yellow and place it in a bag. They obtain blue from Blue River, Kentucky, red from Red Bank, New Jersey, and the rest at the Painted Desert, in Arizona. The skies rumble, and thunder and lightning herald a massive rainfall. Time is running out.

When the rain stops, a pacing Mr. Rembrandt believes it is too late. Tom, still at the Painted Desert, turns into a cannon. He shoots Manfred and the bag of paint toward Rainbow County.

During his flight, Manfred spins, and the bag opens, releasing colors that create a beautiful rainbow. There's still enough paint left over to fill the artist's paint pots, too.

Having saved the day, Tom and Manfred look into the sky to enjoy the whimsical, loopy rainbow the Wonder Dog created.

ROBINSNEST CRUSOE

(Season 2, Episode 12 / First Broadcast December 8, 1958)

Tom Terrific and Manfred the Wonder Dog travel out to sea and end up on a small island where they meet Robinsnest Crusoe, an elderly, ship-wrecked inhabitant.

Tom and Manfred have to pay to stay, as Crusoe runs a string of small islands he calls Robinsnest Rest, a happy haven for tired travelers. But the resort manager is worried. The annual underwater ball game is approaching, but they cannot play. All the team uniforms are in Davey Jones' locker facility, locked away in Crusoe's locker, and someone has stolen the key.

Tom and Manfred hitch a ride on Anchovy Dick, a whale, diving to the ocean floor. They visit Jones' locker facility, but Davey won't open Crusoe's locker without a key. He suggests visiting Locksmith, the key keeper.

The pair is captured by Pittsburgh the Pirate and taken aboard his ship. He has the key, but won't give it up. Why? Because Crusoe won't allow him to play on the team, and if he can't play, no one will.

Manfred kicks a large bell he thinks will bring dinner, but it is a signal to abandon ship. The pirates jump overboard. Our heroes sail to meet Locksmith, but end up in the ocean again. They encounter Anchovy Dick. Tom notices he's rattling. He opens his mouth and Tom find many keys.

One opens Jones' locker, and the uniforms are in play. So is Pittsburgh the Pirate, who is allowed to join the team.

THE EVERLASTING BIRTHDAY PARTY
(Season 2, Episode 13 / First Broadcast December 15, 1958)

Tom Terrific and Manfred the Wonder Dog are on their way home after an adventure, when they discover Isotope Feeny in the road, with a gift-wrapped box. He tells them he is going to an everlasting birthday party.

Manfred becomes excited about the party, but Tom reminds him they have not been invited. Captain Kidney Bean meets them and says he's been invited, too. Mr. Instant suddenly appears. He's headed to the party. Tom and Manfred race home to see if they've received an invitation.

Tom finds an envelope with a message saying he is NOT invited to the party. It's from Crabby Appleton, the host. Tom and Manfred are sad. But Tom ponders, "There's no such thing as an everlasting birthday party."

Sweet Tooth Sam strolls by. He's going to the party. Manfred can't stand it. The ice cream. The cake. He demands they "crash the party."

Tom notices others around them are doing and undoing things. Time moves forward, then back, and repeats. Time has gotten stuck. They head to Appleton's party to see if a solution lurks there.

Crabby has stuck time on his birthday, so it will never end. He makes Tom think it's his imagination, but Tom sees things are still being done and undone. Tom turns into a birthday present Manfred delivers to return to the party. There Tom learns how Crabby made time freeze and fixes it.

Crabby turns one year older, but no wiser.

Gene Deitch holding a copy of the first issue of Pine Comics' *Tom Terrific* series.

TOM TERRIFIC COMIC BOOKS

To compliment the *Tom Terrific* animated series, several issues of a Tom Terrific comic book were published by Pine Comics from 1957 to 1958. Terrytoons possessed a longtime business relationship with Ned L. Pines, principle stockholder and publisher of Literary Enterprises, Inc.

"Shortly after *Tom Terrific* was launched on the *Captain Kangaroo* CBS television network show, we were contracted by Pines Comics to do *Tom Terrific* comic books," Gene Deitch explained. "To fill the pages, we needed to create a special team. Tom Morrison became the editor, as he had plenty of experience putting together the Terrytoons *Mighty Mouse*, *Gandy Goose* comic books for many years. Every animator in the studio jumped into the *Tom Terrific* comic book project."

This included Larz Bourne, Eli Bauer, Bob Kuwahara, Dave Tendlar,

Connie Rasinsky and Art Bartsch.

"I can tell you I personally drew and inked all of the comic book covers myself," Deitch added. "After all, *Tom Terrific* was my character, so I felt I should draw at least a couple of comics stories to set the style."

One of the stories Deitch wrote, drew, inked and lettered was about early space travel. In the story, Tom Terrific turns into a rocket and refers to Manfred the Wonder Dog as "Pupnik." Some of the comic panels from the adventure appear in this chapter.

"I did this story about the time of the first Russian, grapefruit-sized Sputnik," Deitch recalled. "It was big news at the time, now dated and quaint!"

Deitch admits that with his responsibilities regarding the animated cartoon the comic books slipped into the background.

"I was mainly busy as the creative director of the studio, so I lost track of the comic book project, and have only a few beat up copies," he said. "I just came up with faded pages of one story I did, with *Tom Terrific* in an Arabian Nights setup."

Also accompanying the comic book series were other print publications including Wonder Books, coloring book, a vinyl record featuring the *Tom Terrific* theme song performed by Lionel Wilson, and more. Toys and other promotional merchandise also appeared in the consumer market.

Tom Terrific comic book #1

Tom Terrific comic book #2

TOM TERRIFIC COMIC #1
(Pine Comics / Published June 1957)

Contents: Tom and Manfred help Paul Puny get free tickets to the circus. / The world's fastest wallpaper hanger causes problems. / Tom and Manfred go fishing, only to find the river has no water, so Tom transforms into a helicopter and a cyclone to find a thirsty alligator. / Manfred just wants to have a lazy afternoon, but ends up chasing a rabbit and then being chased by a bear. / Tom and Manfred help find an elepharaffe, and Tom turns into a spray gun, an airplane, and an alarm clock to bring the animal to the zoo. / Tom and Manfred are marooned on an island. / Manfred watches Tom help an ungrateful cat from a tree. / Tom and Manfred help find the circus' missing animals. / Manfred watches Tom help an ungrateful cat from a tree. / Crabby Appleton is a dog catcher, trying to catch Manfred, but Tom gets Crabby arrested.

TOM TERRIFIC COMIC #2
(Pine Comics / Published September 1957)

Contents: Facts about the shark sucker, whales, the African lung fish, the oyster, the lobster, and the porcupine fish. / Tom makes some cereal to pep up Manfred, but some mosquitoes eat it, too. / Tom and Manfred are fishing for a prehistoric catfish in the S.S. Cul-de-sac, while Crabby

Tom Terrific comic book #3

Tom Terrific comic book #4

57

Appleton, the world's meanest meanie, causes problems. / Tom takes Manfred back in time to 1709, to warn of a disaster, while Crabby Appleton sneaks along for bad measure. / Flebus gives apples to people, with mixed results. Ends with a 3/4 page joke. / Crabby gives Tom some doggy wash that shrinks Manfred/Coin tossing game.

TOM TERRIFIC COMIC #3

(Pine Comics / Published December 1957)

Contents: Tom helps Manfred stay dry in the rain, but suffers an unexpected consequence. / Tom is not getting mail from his pen pals, so he transforms into a stamp to trace a letter sent to him. / Sidney the elephant is afraid of mice so he asks the king of beasts for advice. / Foolish Fog with Tom Terrific, Manfred the Wonder Dog, Isotope Feeney. / Manfred needs some of his favorite pie to get some energy, but farmer Boodle is out of

Comic book page panels written, illustrated and inked by Gene Deitch, 1957.

berries. / Crabby just finished a correspondence course on how to be a master of disguise, first he's disguised as a bush, but then he has a more sinister plan. / Puzzle page with Tom Terrific and Manfred the Wonder Dog. / Manfred is cold, so Tom turns into a blanket, but Manfred finds another use for a blanket. / A big bone makes Manfred happy. /Manfred wants to be a feared dog.

TOM TERRIFIC COMIC #4
(Pine Comics / Published March 1958)

Contents: Crabby tries to steal Manfred. / Crabby buys the baseball factory and refuses to sell baseballs so no one can play. / Manfred's tail predicts a nice day, but Dr. Instant has other ideas. / Manfred is fooled by Tom once, but not twice. / Gandy Goose story. / Tom and Manfred find a time machine and go back to the Middle Ages, only to find that Crabby Appleton is a mean king. / Sidney the Elephant story. / Gandy Goose story. / Gaston Le Crayon story.

TOM TERRIFIC COMIC #5
(Pine Comics / Published June 1958)

Contents: Tom Terrific and Manfred visit a ranch where animals are branded. / Crabby runs a bubblegum blowing contest, but with a sinister

Tom Terrific comic book #5   *Tom Terrific* comic book #6

purpose. / Visiting the Dog Hall of Fame, Tom and Manfred find a statue that looks like Manfred. / Manfred finds a new place to nap. / Crabby's mean trick with Tom Terrific and Manfred the Wonder Dog. /Sick Sidney

Inside cover page from the *Tom Terrific* comic book series.

story. / Tom discovers Bubblehead Billingsley is hoarding all the soap trying to blow a square bubble. / Tom figures out how to photograph a sleepy dog. / Tom figures he needs to get Manfred back in shape for their next glorious adventure.

TOM TERRIFIC COMIC #6
(Pine Comics / Published September 1958)

Contents: Gaston Le Crayon story. / Tom and Manfred go back in time to the Wild West. / Tom sees the sun is not setting and everything is burning up. / Crabby's strange pooch story. / Sidney the Elephant story. / Connect the dots: Manfred's Rapid Taxi. / After the moon's light goes out, Tom and Manfred investigate. / Maze: Mighty Manfred's Problem. / Crabby sprays Manfred with paint, but Tom helps out.

OTHER TOM TERRIFIC PUBLICATIONS
(Miscellaneous)

Tom Terrific appeared in two editions of picture books published by Crosby Newell and Arthur Bartsch's Wonder Books. The Wonder Book titles included *Tom Terrific with Manfred the Wonder Dog* published in 1958, and *Tom Terrific's Greatest Adventure,* published in 1959.

Tom Terrific appeared in the pages of two Whitman Coloring Books, *Tom Terrific with Manfred the Wonder Dog* published in 1958, and *The Terrytoons Coloring Book*, published in 1970, which featured Tom with

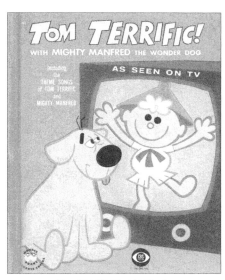
Tom Terrific Wonder Book.

Tom Terrific Wonder Book.

the characters Deputy Dawg, Hashimoto San and Heckle and Jeckle.

Golden Records released a *Tom Terrific* audio and music became a 78rpm record in 1960. The small vinyl disc featured the voice of Lionel Wilson with Don Elliott and the Skip Jacks.

Merchandise also included some *Tom Terrific* toys and *Tom Terrific and Manfred the Wonder Dog* puppets.

Tom Terrific coloring book.

Terrytoons coloring book.

"Of course, Manfred—the ocean!" Tom cried, hugging the sleepy dog. "Oh, what would I ever do without you! I'll be an ocean liner and you will be the captain." With a *whirr*, a *bong-a-long*, four spins and a triple twist, Tom was a great ocean liner with two smokestacks, sailing across the ocean.

Tom Terrific Wonder Book page.

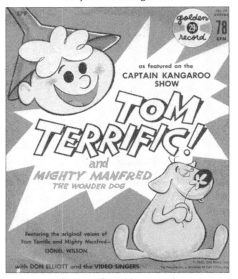
Tom Terrific Golden Record.

① HE ANNOUNCES WHAT HE'LL BE —

② HE SQUINCHES ALL UP —

③ — AND WIGGLES INTO HIS NEW SHAPE! (THE SPIRAL WHIRLS AROUND HIM)

TOM'S AMAZING TRANSFORMATIONS

Tom Terrific wasn't averse to change. In fact, he welcomed it. In the two seasons of the program, Tom turned into something 129 times. What follows is a complete directory of every amazing Tom Terrific transformation, in which episode it occurred, and why he became it.

Accompanying pages reproduce images from every transformation in random order. Can you match the list to the item pictured? Place a little check mark beside each listing and on each graphic as you locate them.

Sometimes Tom changed into identical things, such as a tree, bee, flea or cat. If you find one, you can mark them all. But cars come in different models, and birds in various species, so these are unique. By process of elimination, you should figure them all out.

AIRPLANE - Tom Terrific turns into an airplane in the opening credits of season one of Tom Terrific. Why? To show one of the many things he can turn into for viewers of the show.

AIRPLANE - Tom Terrific turns into a flying jet plane in "Scrambled Dinosaur Eggs." Why? To pursue Manfred the Wonder Dog, who is flying on the back of a prehistoric Rhamphorhynchus.

AIRPLANE - Tom Terrific turns into an airplane in "Who Stole the North Pole?" Why? To transport he and Manfred the Wonder Dog to the

North Pole on a mission to find out who took the pole.

AIRPLANE - Tom Terrific turns into a mail plane in "The Missing Mail Mystery." Why? To take he and Manfred the Wonder Dog around the globe to see why his young pen pals have not been writing to him.

BALLOON - Tom Terrific turns into a balloon in the opening credits of season two of Tom Terrific. Why? To show one of the many things he can turn into for viewers of the show.

BALLOON - Tom Terrific turns into a helium balloon in "Captain Kidney Bean." Why? To create lift in the chest he is trapped inside at the bottom of the sea. The buoyancy brings it to the surface where Tom is free to escape.

BALLOON - Tom Terrific turns into a hot air balloon in "Scrambled Dinosaur Eggs." Why? To lift he and Manfred the Wonder Dog away from a volcano which is about to erupt.

BASEBALL GLOVE - Tom Terrific turns into a baseball glove in the opening credits of season two of Tom Terrific. Why? To show one of the many things he can turn into for viewers of the show.

BASEBALL GLOVE - Tom Terrific turns into a baseball glove in "Track Meet, Well Done." Why? To catch a baseball headed his way, knocked out of the park by a bully known as Musclehead.

BEE - Tom Terrific turns into a bumble bee in the opening credits of season one of Tom Terrific. Why? To show one of the many things he can turn into for viewers of the show.

BEE - Tom Terrific turns into a bee in "The Gravity Maker." Why? To fly up into Isotope Feeney's Ivory Tower, where the scientist is experimenting on Manfred the Wonder Dog with anti-gravity devices.

BIRD - Tom Terrific turns into a bird in "The Pill of Smartness." Why? To fly inside the Egyptian sphinx to see if Crabby Appleton is inside plotting evil.

BIRD - Tom Terrific turns into a pelican in "Who Stole the North Pole?" Why? To follow a formation of geese in order to establish direction. The geese inform him they are flying south. Thus, Tom knows that to reach north he must travel in the opposite direction.

BIRD - Tom Terrific turns into an eagle in "Go West, Young Manfred." Why? To fly he and Manfred the Wonder Dog to a stream to pan for gold.

BIRD - Tom Terrific turns into an owl in "The Nasty Knight." Why? Tom is seeking a solution, so imagines that becoming a "wise old owl" will do the trick.

BUCKET - Tom Terrific turns into a bucket full of water in "Instant Tantrums." Why? To toss onto Manfred the Wonder Dog to get him to snap out of a tantrum.

BLOTTER - Tom Terrific turns into a big blotter during a rainstorm in "The End of Rainbows." Why? So he can suck up all the colors at Arizona's Painted Desert and get them to Mr. Rembrandt, the artist who paints rainbows.

BOAT - Tom Terrific turns into a toy wind-up, ocean liner in "Snowy Picture." Why? So he can transport Manfred, via ocean, to their North Pole destination.

BONE - Tom Terrific turns into a dog bone in the opening credits of season two of Tom Terrific. Why? To show one of the many things he can turn into for viewers of the show.

BONE - Tom Terrific turns into a dog bone in "The Pill of Smartness." Why? So the smell will attract Manfred so that the Wonder Dog can find the hidden room Tom is in, and rescue him.

BONE - Tom Terrific turns into a dog bone in "The Missing Mail Mystery." Why? To attract Manfred the Wonder Dog to his location in order to set him free from Crabby Appleton's hideout.

BUGLE - Tom Terrific turns into a bugle in "Go West, Young Manfred." Why? To sound a warning to Indians who have encircled a wagon train, tricking them into thinking the Calvary is on the way, causing them to flee.

BUTTERFLY - Tom Terrific turns into a butterfly in "Crabby Park." Why? To fly over the trees in Crabby Appleton's park to find Manfred the Wonder Dog, from whom he was separated.

CALENDAR - Tom Terrific turns into a calendar in "Crabby's Park." Why? To change the season to fall. Crabby Appleton has stolen all the trees to create his own park, but has no desire to keep them, or grab a rake, when a million leaves begin to fall.

CAMEL - Tom Terrific turns into a camel in "The Silly Sandman." Why? To transport he and Manfred the Wonder Dog to the Sierra Dessert.

CANNON - Tom Terrific turns into a circus cannon in "The End of Rainbows." Why? So he can shoot Manfred the Wonder Dog out of the cannon, with a bag of colors, to quickly get them to Mr. Rembrandt, who paints rainbows.

CAR - Tom Terrific turns into a "Chitty Chitty Bang Bang" type sports car in "Snowy Picture." Why? To transport he and Manfred the Wonder Dog to the Empire State Building in New York.

CAR - Tom Terrific turns into a custom roadster in "Snowy Picture." Why? To transport he and Manfred the Wonder Dog to the Empire State Building in New York.

CAR - Tom Terrific turns into a sleek, Porche-like, sports car in "Snowy Picture." Why? To transport he and Manfred the Wonder Dog to the Empire State Building in New York.

CAR - Tom Terrific turns into an invisible racing car in "Isotope Feeny's Foolish Fog." Why? Tom determines that if he is invisible, Isotope Feeny's Foolish Fog will not affect him. The race car provides him with quick transportation to the city, to rescue the citizens who are under a cloud of foolishness.

CAR - Tom Terrific appears as a two-door, hardtop at the beginning of "The Everlasting Birthday Party." Why? Because he is driving Manfred the Wonder Dog home from another great adventure.

CAT - Tom Terrific turns into a small cat in "Snowy Picture." Why? To get Manfred the Wonder Dog to wake up and chase him. Manfred wakes up, but is frightened of the kitty, so he's the one running, away, that is.

CAT - Tom Terrific turns into a cat in "The Big Dog Show-Off." Why? To get Manfred the Wonder Dog to chase him so the judges at the dog show see how active his pooch can be.

CHARIOT - Tom Terrific turns into an Egyptian chariot in "The Pill of Smartness." Why? To fly he and Manfred the Wonder Dog to the sphinx in Egypt to find a pill that makes one wise.

CLOCK - Tom Terrific turns into a time clock in "Captain Kidney Bean." Why? By turning into a clock that can change time, Tom can transport he and Manfred back in time, to the days of pirates on the high seas.

CLOCK - Tom Terrific turns into a clock that ticks backward in "Go West, Young Manfred." Why? To transport he and Manfred the Wonder Dog to California during the days of the Great Gold Rush.

COMPASS - Tom Terrific turns into a compass in "Who Stole the North Pole?" Why? To find out the direction of Crabby Appleton's secret hideout.

CONTROL MACHINE - Tom Terrific turns into a computer-like, upright, control machine in "Crabby Appleton's Dragon." Why? To trick Crabby Appleton in order to subdue him. In Appleton's absence, Tom replaces Appleton's control station with himself.

DAM - Tom Terrific turns into a dam in "Crabby's Park." Why? To block a waterfall, so Manfred the Wonder Dog, who is trapped in the flow of a river, won't go over it.

DICTIONARY - Tom Terrific turns into an Eskimo dictionary in "Snowy Picture." Why? He receives a fan letter from an Eskimo at the North Pole, and, not knowing the language, decides to look it up.

DISH - Tom Terrific turns into a rolling dish in "The Flying Sorcerer." Why? It's part of a riddle he must solve, a portion of which involves a rolling dinner plate.

DOOR - Tom Terrific turns into a large, wooden door with handles, and hinges, in "The Nasty Knight." Why? To bring galloping Sir Nasty Knight to a screeching halt and confuse him, during an arena battle.

DRAIN - Tom Terrific turns into a large, bathtub drain at the bottom of the ocean in "Crabby Appleton's Dragon." Why? To suck the dogfish circling Manfred on the surface to the bottom, away from him.

ELEVATOR - Tom Terrific turns into an elevator in "Snowy Picture." Why? To transport he and Manfred the Wonder Dog to the top of the Empire State Building, in order to fix a television transmission tower.

FAN - Tom Terrific turns into a fan in "Isotope Feeny's Foolish Fog." Why? To blow Isotope Feeny's Foolish Fog back at the fiend, rendering him foolish, thereby disabling him from being a threat to society.

FEATHER - Tom Terrific turns into a feather in "Elephant Stew." Why? To soften his landing after being tossed through the air by an elephant.

FISH - Tom Terrific turns into a swordfish in "The Nasty Knight." Why? Tom is bored, and, seeking adventure, became a swordfish so he could fight a giant whale. After his transformation, he reverted back to himself, realizing he would need an ocean to achieve this, and as he said, "there's no ocean around here."

FISH - Tom Terrific turns into a flying fish in "Robinsnest Crusoe" Why? To fly Manfred the Wonder Dog out to sea to a desert island.

FLEA - Tom Terrific turns into a flea in the opening credits of season two of Tom Terrific. Why? To show one of the many things he can turn into for viewers of the show.

FLEA - Tom Terrific turns into a flea in "The Flying Sorcerer." Why? Because Tom has lost Manfred the Wonder Dog, and dogs always find their fleas.

FROG - Tom Terrific turns into a frog in "Crabby Appleton's Dragon." Why? To swim beneath the ocean surface, unnoticed, gaining entry to Crabby Appleton's secret island laboratory.

GEIGER COUNTER - Tom Terrific turns into a Geiger Counter in "Captain Kidney Bean." Why? To be able to detect a buried treasure chest Captain Kidney Bean has hidden on Bloodshot Island.

GIANT - Tom Terrific turns into a giant in "Crabby Appleton's Dragon." Why? To be tall enough to peek inside Crabby Appleton's control room, from a few floors below, in an open shaft.

GLOBE - Tom Terrific turns into a globe of the Earth in the opening credits of season one of Tom Terrific. Why? To show one of the many things he can turn into for viewers of the show.

GLOBE - Tom Terrific turns into a globe of the Earth in "The Silly

Sandman." Why? To show The Sandman, who is responsible for children going to sleep, how half the planet is in daylight, while the other half is at night.

GOAT - Tom Terrific turns into a sure-footed goat in "The Prince Frog." Why? So he can navigate the rocky terrain of a mountainous peak.

GROCERY CART - Tom Terrific turns into a grocery cart in "The Million Manfred Mystery." Why? To run to the grocery store to get Manfred the Wonder Dog a jar of peanut butter.

HELICOPTER - Tom Terrific turns into a helicopter in "The Nasty Knight." Why? Tom needs to get he and Feeble Fred off the arena ground fast, as Sir Nasty Knight, with lance in hand, gallops toward them on horseback.

HORSE - Tom Terrific turns into a horse in "The Nasty Knight." Why? Feeble Fred must battle Sir Nasty Knight in the arena. He has no horse to ride, so Tom accommodates.

IGLOO - Tom Terrific turns into an igloo in "Who Stole the North Pole." Why? To cover Manfred the Wonder Dog to protect him from a snowy avalanche triggered by Crabby Appleton.

KEY - Tom Terrific turns into a golden key in the opening credits of season two of Tom Terrific. Why? To show one of the many things he can turn into for viewers of the show.

LIGHTBULB - Tom Terrific turns into a lightbulb in the opening credits of season two of Tom Terrific. Why? To show one of the many things he can turn into for viewers of the show.

LIGHTBULB - Tom Terrific turns into a lightbulb in "The Great Calendar Mystery." Why? To throw some light inside Nathaniel Annual's Calendar Factory to see what Crabby Appleton is up to.

LIGHTNING BOLT - Tom Terrific turns into a lightning bolt in "The Great Calendar Mystery." Why? To cause rain and spoil Crabby Appleton's day at the Dandyland.

LIGHTNING BOLT - Tom Terrific turns into a streak of lightning in "The End of Rainbows." Why? So he can go quickly to Yellowstone, Wyoming, like a streak of lightning.

LOUDSPEAKER - Tom Terrific turns into a giant loudspeaker in "The Million Manfred Mystery." Why? So the Martians that abducted Manfred the Wonder Dog from the tree house will hear Tom's message to return him.

MAGIC CARPET - Tom Terrific turns into a magic carpet in "The Flying Sorcerer." Why? To transport he and Manfred the Wonder Dog back to ancient Bagdad and the time of sorcery and the Arabian Knights.

MAGNET - Tom Terrific turns into a large magnet in "The Nasty

Knight." Why? So Tom, as a magnet, can pull off Sir Nasty Knight's armor, making it an even match in the arena for his opponent, Feeble Fred, who is running about unarmed in a loincloth.

MAGNIFYING GLASS - Tom Terrific turns into a large magnifying glass in "Sweet Tooth Sam." Why? To shoot a beam of heat at Sweet Tooth Sam's gun belt, setting off all the bullets.

MAILBOX - Tom Terrific turns into a large mailbox in "The Missing Mail Mystery." Why? To receive what he believes will be a large volume of fan mail delivered by the postman.

MATTRESS - Tom Terrific turns into an inner-spring mattress in "Isotope Feeny's Foolish Fog." Why? To cushion Manfred the Wonder Dog's landing, after he falls out of Tom Terrific's treehouse headquarters.

METEOR - Tom Terrific turns into a meteor in "Moon Over Manfred." Why? To journey into space and find a replacement for the Man in the Moon, who quit his job and moved.

MIRROR - Tom Terrific turns into a large mirror in "Scrambled Dinosaur Eggs." Why? So the dinosaurs hiding in a cave will see themselves, be frightened, and stay in the cave. It doesn't work, so Tom bends the glass to produce scary images.

MOTORCYCLE - Tom Terrific turns into a motorcycle with a siren in "Captain Kidney Bean." Why? To provide fast transportation to trail Captain Kidney Bean, and his passenger Manfred the Wonder Dog, back to the pirate's ship.

MOUSE - Tom Terrific turns into a mouse in "The Pill of Smartness." Why? To become small enough to navigate a small tunnel inside the Egyptian sphinx, while searching for the Pill of Smartness.

MOUSE - Tom Terrific turns into a mouse in "The Gravity Maker." Why? To gain access into Isotope Feeney's Ivory Tower, where the scientist is experimenting on Manfred the Wonder Dog with anti-gravity devices.

MOUSE - Tom Terrific turns into a mouse in "Elephant Stew." Why? To scare an angry elephant into submission.

MUMMY - Tom Terrific turns into an Egyptian mummy in "The Pill of Smartness." Why? To be able to read hieroglyphics on an interior wall of the Sphinx.

NEST - Tom Terrific turns into a dinosaur nest in "Scrambled Dinosaur Eggs." Why? To see if he can get a dinosaur to lay an egg. That way he can hatch a dinosaur at the Museum of Natural History to replace the dinosaur (skeleton) Manfred broke.

PARACHUTE - Tom Terrific turns into a parachute in "Elephant Stew." Why? To allow he and Manfred the Wonder Dog a safe landing after departing a rocket ship.

PEANUT BUTTER - Tom Terrific turns into a jar of peanut butter in "The Million Manfred Mystery." Why? To attract Manfred the Wonder Dog, as his faithful companion loves peanut butter and the pooch is missing.

PEPPER SHAKER - Tom Terrific turns into a pepper shaker in "Crabby Appleton's Dragon." Why? To cause an oyster to sneeze, releasing a pearl from inside. Tom believes the pearl causes the creature pain and wants to help.

POGO STICK - Tom Terrific turns into a pogo stick in "Sweet Tooth Sam." Why? He and Manfred fall from a cliff, and Tom transforms into the pogo stick for Manfred to hold. Instead of an impact of disaster, Tom springs he and his dog to safety.

POSTAGE STAMP - Tom Terrific turns into a postage stamp in "The Missing Mail Mystery." Why? To attach himself to a letter and go through the mail to see what is blocking him from receiving letters at home.

PRESENT - Tom Terrific turns into a birthday present in "The Everlasting Birthday Party." Why? So Manfred the Wonder Dog can deliver him to Crabby Appleton on his birthday, to gain knowledge as to how the villain has frozen time, and unfreeze it.

PUNCHING BAG - Tom Terrific turns into a punching bag in "Track Meet, Well Done." Why? To absorb the impact when bully Musclehead throws a punch at Tom.

RABBIT - Tom Terrific turns into a rabbit in "The Pill of Smartness." Why? To become small enough to navigate a small tunnel inside the Egyptian sphinx, while searching for the Pill of Smartness.

RADIO WAVE - Tom Terrific turns into a radio wave in "Moon Over Manfred." Why? So he can transport he and Manfred the Wonder Dog to the surface of the moon.

ROCKET - Tom Terrific turns into a rocket in "Elephant Stew." Why? To transport he and Manfred the Wonder Dog to Africa.

ROCKET - Tom Terrific turns into a rocket in the opening credits of season two of Tom Terrific. Why? To show one of the many things he can turn into for viewers of the show.

ROCKET - Tom Terrific turns into a rocket in "Moon Over Manfred." Why? So he and Manfred the Wonder Dog can go to the moon to determine why it has gone dark.

ROLLER COASTER CAR - Tom Terrific turns into a roller coaster car in "The End of Rainbows." Why? So he can transport Manfred the Wonder Dog, atop a rainbow, to find its end, and perhaps, a pot of gold.

ROPE - Tom Terrific turns into a rope in "The Pill of Smartness." Why?

To lasso Manfred the Wonder Dog, during a fall from a statue of Cleopatra, in the Great Sphinx of Egypt.

RUG - Tom Terrific turns into a throw rug in "Captain Kidney Bean." Why? So he can throw himself under a door to escape the room, as a prisoner of Captain Kidney Bean.

SADDLEBAG - Tom Terrific turns into a saddlebag in "Go West, Young Manfred." Why? To carry gold nuggets, and hitch a ride with the Pony Express, during the Great California Gold Rush.

SAIL - Tom Terrific turns into a sail in "Robinsnest Crusoe." Why? To provide a sail for an abandoned pirate ship he and Manfred have taken over.

SAUCER AND CUP - Tom Terrific turns into a coffee cup atop a "flying" saucer in "The End of Rainbows." Why? So he can transport Manfred the Wonder Dog to Yellowstone, Wyoming.

SAXOPHONE - Tom Terrific turns into a saxophone in the opening credits of season two of Tom Terrific. Why? To show one of the many things he can turn into for viewers of the show.

SHIP - Tom Terrific turns into a phantom sailing ship in "Captain Kidney Bean." Why? So he can trail Captain Kidney Bean's pirate vessel, and recover the stolen treasure chest that belongs to sick, old sailors.

SHIP - Tom Terrific turns into sailing ship in the opening credits of season two of Tom Terrific. Why? To show one of the many things he can turn into for viewers of the show.

SHOES - Tom Terrific turns into a pair of magic shoes in "Track Meet, Well Done." Why? To convince a group of little kids that they can win any athletic event, as the shoes will make them jump higher and run faster. But the shoes he gives them are nothing special. It's their confidence that allows them to win.

SNOWBALL - Tom Terrific turns into a rolling snowball in "Who Stole the North Pole?" Why? So he can chase after fleeing Crabby Appleton, who has put Manfred into a harness, using him as a sled dog.

SLIDE - Tom Terrific turns into an extra-long, playground slide in "Instant Tantrums." Why? To allow Manfred the Wonder Dog, who was high atop a tree, a safe and quick way down to terra firma.

SLIDE - Tom Terrific turns into a standard playground slide in "The End of Rainbows." Why? So Manfred the Wonder Dog, who has fallen off a rainbow, can slide safely to the ground.

SMOKE - Tom Terrific turns into a floating trail of smoke in "Track Meet, Well Done." Why? To escape an athletic locker he was trapped in and exit through a vent.

SPECK - Tom Terrific turns into a speck in "The Pill of Smartness."

Why? To become small enough to navigate a very narrow tunnel inside the Egyptian sphinx. It's possible Tom has turned into a flea, but he never identifies what he has become, and no tiny wings are visible.

SPOTLIGHT - Tom Terrific turns into a spotlight in "The Big Dog Show-Off." Why? To throw a spotlight on Manfred the Wonder Dog at the dog show.

STAGECOACH - Tom Terrific turns into a stagecoach in "Go West, Young Manfred." Why? To transport he and Manfred the Wonder Dog back to the days of the California Gold Rush.

STEAM - Tom Terrific turns into a cloud of steam in "The Silly Sandman." Why? To lift he and Manfred the Wonder Dog aloft to reach the top of the Matterhorn, in Switzerland.

SUBWAY TRAIN - Tom Terrific turns into a subway train in "The Great Calendar Mystery." Why? To transport he and Manfred the Wonder Dog to Nathaniel Annual's Calendar Factory.

SUNLAMP - Tom Terrific turns into a super sunlamp in "The Prince Frog." Why? So he can create light, and heat, to make the grass grow in The Dark Forest.

TANK - Tom Terrific turns into an armored tank in "The Nasty Knight." Why? Feeble Fred has no armor to wear in battle against Sir Nasty Knight. Tom becomes a tank to be his armor.

TELEPHONE BOOTH - Tom Terrific turns into a telephone booth in "The Great Calendar Mystery." Why? So Crabby Appleton answers the phone, so Tom can give him a message that if he returns the holidays and weekends he stole from the calendar, it will stop raining.

TELESCOPE - Tom Terrific turns into a telescope in "Moon Over Manfred." Why? So Manfred the Wonder Dog can take a look at the moon to determine why it has gone dark.

TELEVISION - Tom Terrific turns into a television set in "The Pill of Smartness." Why? Manfred the Wonder Dog's favorite TV program is about to air, and with no television nearby, Tom accommodates.

TELEGRAM - Tom Terrific turns into a telegram in "Track Meet, Well Done." Why? To slip under Musclehead's front door, and give him a message to halt his nasty policy of banning little kids from playing on his baseball team.

TRAFFIC SIGNAL - Tom Terrific turns into traffic signal in the opening credits of season two of Tom Terrific. Why? To show one of the many things he can turn into for viewers of the show.

TRAIN - Tom Terrific turns into a diesel train in the opening credits of season one of Tom Terrific. Why? To show one of the many things he can turn into for viewers of the show.

TREE - Tom Terrific turns into a tree in the opening credits of season one of Tom Terrific. Why? To show one of the many things he can turn into for viewers of the show.

TREE - Tom Terrific turns into a tree in "The Nasty Knight." Why? Tom doesn't turn into just any tree, but a tree in King Arthur's Court, so he can be transported there with Manfred on an adventure.

TREE - Tom Terrific turns into a tree in "Crabby's Park." Why? Appleton has been stealing all the trees. Tom figures if he turns into one Crabby will take him to the missing forestry.

TUB - Tom Terrific turns into a bathtub in "The Pill of Smartness." Why? So the water will snap Manfred the Wonder Dog out of a hypnotic state cast upon him by Crabby Appleton.

UMBRELLA - Tom Terrific turns into an umbrella in "Instant Tantrums." Why? To shield Manfred, who is wearing a collar holding a box of tantrum powder. If the powder gets wet, it will go off and cause everyone in the town to throw a tantrum.

VACCUM CLEANER - Tom Terrific turns into a vacuum cleaner in "The End of Rainbows." Why? To suck up the color yellow at Yellowstone National Park, and give it to Mr. Rembrandt, the rainbow artist.

WAND - Tom Terrific turns into a magician's wand in "The Prince Frog." Why? So Manfred the Wonder Dog can say the magic words and transport he and Tom Terrific to fairyland.

WEATHER INDICATOR - Tom Terrific turns into a weather indicator dial in "Instant Tantrums." Why? So he can change the weather from impending rain to very dry, and stop Mr. Instant from releasing Tantrum Powder that rains down on the town below.

WHALE - Tom Terrific turns into a whale in "Snowy Picture." Why? So he can swim to the North Pole with Manfred transported on his back.

WINDMILL - Tom Terrific turns into a Dutch windmill in "The Missing Mail Mystery." Why? To fly he and Manfred the Wonder Dog to the country of Holland.

YODEL - Tom Terrific turns into a yodel in "The Silly Sandman." Why? So he, in the Sierra Dessert, can call out to The Sandman, who is atop the Matterhorn, in Switzerland.

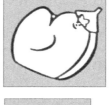

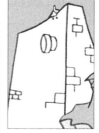

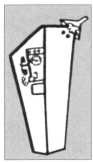

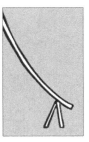
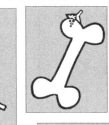

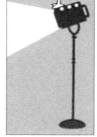

PEANUT BUTTER

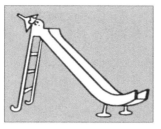

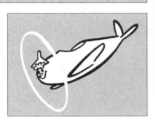

79

EASTER EGGS AND TRIVIA

Accompanying Tom Terrific's amazing transformations are many other amusing things to see and hear in the series. Some are obvious, but many fly by like a raging locomotive.

Manfred the Mighty Wonder Dog undergoes a few transformations, or at least, it appears so. Tom tries to disguise Manfred as a dragon in one episode. In another, Witch One briefly changes Manfred into a giant rabbit. He becomes an Indian chief in a tale about the Wild West. There are a couple of others left for you to find.

The giant wearing a New York Giant(s) baseball cap.

Tom Terrific delved in satire for adults. When Tom and Manfred climb the beanstalk to face the giant, he's wearing a New York Giants baseball cap. The depiction of Italy as a boot in one episode is a throwback to what geography teachers of yesteryear told their students. There are humorous references to The Lone Ranger in another adventure.

Tom Terrific had a unique way of expressing amazement in words. His expressions were literally all over the map.

Instead of saying, "Holy cow," he would shout "Holyoke, Massachusetts," for example. The locations could be anywhere from Paint Pot, Idaho, to Chicago, Illinois. There are many in the series, so when watching, keep your ears open.

Did Tom Terrific ever try to change into something, but couldn't? Yes, a helicopter. He tried this in "Go West, Young Manfred." The period was the Old West, and the helicopter had not been invented yet.

While Tom changed 5 times on average in an episode (not including the credits), the one adventure depicting the least amount of transformations is "The Everlasting Birthday Party." In the story opening, Tom is already a car traveling down the road, so he is not seen changing. Near the end of the episode, he turns into a birthday present. Thus, only one transformation is depicted.

There is one thing never identified that Tom became. It was in "The Pill of Smartness," where he travels inside a tunnel that grows increasingly narrower. He becomes a tiny speck. It might be a flea. But, it's *another* great *Tom Terrific* mystery!

44220665R00046

Made in the USA
Middletown, DE
04 May 2019